YAKALOU MEDIA

Are You Mentally Ok?

Let's Find Out With These 100 Eye-opening Yes Or No Questions On Your Mental Health

Contents

Disclaimer

This book is designed to provide information only. This information is provided and sold with the knowledge that the publisher and author do not offer any legal or other professional advice. In the case of a need for any such expertise, consult with the appropriate professional.

This book does not contain all the information available on the subject. This book has not been created to be specific to any individual's or organization's situation or needs. Every effort has been made to make this book as accurate as possible. However, there may be typographical and/or content errors. Therefore, this book should serve only as a general guide, not as the ultimate source of subject information.

This book contains information that might be dated and is intended only to educate and entertain. Regarding any loss or damage allegedly suffered or alleged to have occurred as a result of the information in this book, either directly or indirectly, the author and publisher shall have no liability or responsibility to any person or entity.

I

Before Everything

Introduction

Have you ever paused to consider the state of your mental health? In the hustle and bustle of daily life, it's easy to overlook the importance of mental well-being. Yet, it's as crucial as physical health. "Are You Mentally OK?" is not just a book; it's a journey toward understanding and nurturing your mental state.

Imagine this: What if you could uncover the hidden aspects of your mind with just a simple 'yes' or 'no'? Doesn't that sound intriguing and, perhaps, a little exciting? This book is designed to guide you through that exploration. Each question is a stepping stone toward self-awareness, a tool to help you understand the complex workings of your mind.

But why should you care? Why is it important to check in with your mental health regularly? The answers lie within the fabric of our daily lives. How we think, feel, and react to situations significantly impacts our overall happiness and quality of life. This book offers a mirror to reflect on your inner emotional and mental state, a chance to pause and ponder.

Are you managing stress effectively? Do you feel emotionally balanced? How is your self-esteem shaping your life choices? These are not just questions; they're keys to unlocking a deeper understanding of yourself. Through straightforward, yes-or-no questions, you'll embark on a path of self-discovery, peeling back layers to reveal a clearer picture of your mental and emotional well-being.

Remember, acknowledging and understanding your mental state is the first step toward positive change. As you turn the pages of this book, allow yourself to be open, honest, and a little vulnerable. What you discover might just be the catalyst for transformation, leading you toward a healthier, more fulfilled life. So, are you ready to begin this journey? Let's find out together.

What Will You Learn in This Book

As you venture into the pages of "Are You Mentally OK?" you're embarking on a journey of self-awareness and discovery. But what exactly will you learn from this journey? How will this book help you understand the nuances of your mental well-being?

This book is more than just a collection of questions; it's a compass that guides you through the intricate landscape of your mind. You will learn to identify the subtle signs of stress and anxiety that often go unnoticed. Have you ever wondered why certain situations make you uncomfortable or why your energy levels fluctuate so much? Through simple yet profound questions, you'll begin to uncover these mysteries.

Moreover, the journey through these pages will illuminate aspects of your emotional health. How do you really feel about your life? Are there hidden emotions you've been avoiding? It's often the simplest questions that bring the most significant insights. By answering these questions honestly, you'll learn to recognize and embrace your emotional states, leading to a better understanding of yourself.

word of warning

But there's a word of warning. This book is not a magic solution. It's a tool for reflection and self-examination. The journey of mental health is deeply personal and varies from one individual to another. While these questions can guide you, they are not definitive diagnoses or solutions to your challenges. They are, however, stepping stones toward seeking further help if needed.

What's more, the path to self-discovery can be uncomfortable. It might challenge your current perceptions and push you out of your comfort zone. Are you ready to face the truths that lie within you? The journey may be unsettling at times, but the rewards of self-awareness and inner peace are invaluable.

In conclusion, this book offers you a mirror to reflect on your mental health and a chance to pause and reflect. It encourages you to ask the hard questions and confront aspects of your life you might have ignored. Through this process, you'll gain a clearer understanding of your mental landscape, empowering you to take steps toward a healthier, more balanced life. The journey starts with a question, and the answers lie within you.

The "Yes or No Questions Concept"

Welcome to the heart of our book, where the real adventure begins! But hold on, before we dive into the fun part, let's take a moment to understand the concept of "Yes or No Questions." What makes these simple questions so powerful, and how can they help you on your journey to better mental health?

"Yes or No Questions" are straightforward, requiring just a single-word answer—either 'yes' or 'no'. But don't let their simplicity fool you. These questions are crafted to cut through the noise and clutter of our busy minds, getting straight to the point. Have you ever been overwhelmed by your thoughts when trying to understand your feelings? These questions bypass that confusion, offering a clear path to your inner truths.

The beauty of this approach lies in its directness. It forces us to confront realities we often overlook. For instance, asking yourself, "Do I feel happy today?" demands an immediate and instinctive response. There's no room for maybe or long-winded explanations. Just a simple 'yes' or 'no' can reveal a lot about your current state of mind.

But here's where it gets interesting. Each 'yes' or 'no' you give is a piece of the puzzle that is your mental health. Imagine these answers as clues that guide you toward a deeper understanding of yourself. Are you often saying 'no' to questions about happiness or fulfillment? What does that tell you about the changes you might need to make?

Now, as we proceed, remember that these questions are not judgments. They are tools for self-reflection. Answering 'no' to a question about feeling content doesn't mean you've failed; it means you've identified an area for growth. It's about being honest with yourself, even when it's tough.

So, are you ready to embark on this journey of discovery with simple yet profound 'yes' or 'no' questions? The answers you find may surprise you, challenge you, and, most importantly, help you grow. As we move forward, embrace the simplicity, honesty, and clarity these questions bring. Let's begin this exciting and enlightening adventure together!

The Rules of the "Yes or No Questions" Game

As we embark on this exciting journey with the "Yes or No Questions" game, it's essential to establish some ground rules. These rules are not just guidelines; they are the pillars that will support you as you navigate through the insightful world of self-discovery. Are you ready to explore the rules that will make this experience both meaningful and transformative?

First and foremost, honesty is key. The game's essence lies in your ability to be truthful with yourself. When you face a question, it might be tempting to respond with what you think you should say or what seems like the 'right' answer. But here's the catch: there is no right or wrong answer. The only thing that matters is your truth. So, can you promise yourself to be honest, even if the truth might be uncomfortable?

Next, let's talk about instinct. These questions are designed to capture your first, unfiltered response. Why? Because often, our initial reactions are the most telling. They are unclouded by overthinking or rationalization. When a question is posed, listen to that immediate voice inside you—that gut feeling. It's your inner self speaking. Are you willing to trust your instincts and go with your first response?

Now, consider the environment. Where you play this game matters. Find a space where you feel safe and undisturbed. It could be a cozy corner of your room, a park bench, or anywhere you can be at ease with your thoughts. Are you ready to find that special spot where you can be alone with your thoughts, away from distractions?

Additionally, pacing is crucial. There's no need to rush through the questions. This is not a race; it's a journey of exploration. Take your time with each question, allowing yourself to fully process and understand your response. Can you give yourself the gift of time to reflect and ponder each question thoughtfully?

Lastly, remember that this is not a diagnostic tool. The "Yes or No Questions" game is a method of self-exploration, not a professional evaluation. It's about gaining insights into your mental state, not about labeling or diagnosing. So, are you ready to use these questions as a means to understand yourself better, not as a judgment on your character or abilities?

In conclusion, these rules are here to guide you toward a meaningful and honest engagement with the "Yes or No Questions" game. By following them, you're setting yourself up for a journey that's not only enlightening but also respectful of your mental and emotional well-being. So, are you ready to play by these rules and uncover the layers of your inner self? Let's begin this journey with an open heart and mind.

How to Interpret the Result of Your "Yes or No Answers"

As you progress through the "Yes or No Questions" game, you'll accumulate a series of answers that paint a picture of your current mental state. But how do you make sense of these answers? How can the number of 'yeses' or 'noes' guide you toward a deeper understanding of your mental well-being? This chapter is dedicated to unraveling the meaning behind your responses and what they signify in your journey toward self-awareness.

The "Yes"

First, let's consider the balance of your answers. If you find yourself answering 'yes' to most questions, especially those related to positive aspects of mental health, like feeling content, managing stress well, or having healthy self-esteem, it indicates a generally positive state of mind. But what does it really mean to have more 'yes' answers? It suggests that you are on a path where your mental health is being nurtured and supported. However, remember, this is not a final verdict. Life is dynamic, and so is our mental state.

The "No"

On the flip side, if 'no' seems to be the predominant answer, particularly to questions that reflect positive mental health, it's a gentle nudge. It indicates areas in your life that might need more attention and care. Does this mean you should be worried? Not necessarily. Instead, view it as an opportunity for growth and self-improvement. It's a starting point for deeper exploration and perhaps a signal to seek additional support if needed.

The Mixed

Now, what about the questions where your answers were mixed? This is where the beauty of self-exploration lies. Life isn't black and white, and neither is our mental health. A mix of 'yes' and 'no' answers reflects the complexities of our emotional and mental landscape. It shows that while some areas of your life are thriving, others might need more nurturing. Can you embrace this complexity and see it as a map guiding you toward areas that need more attention?

Remember, these results are not a judgment. They are reflective indicators, signposts that help you understand where you are in your mental health journey. This understanding is the first step toward making positive changes. Whether it's seeking professional help, talking to a loved one, or simply taking time for self-care, your answers can guide your next steps.

In conclusion, interpreting the results of the "Yes or No Questions" game is about understanding your mental landscape. It's a process of uncovering, discovering, and, most importantly, accepting where you are right now. Each 'yes' and 'no' is a piece of your unique puzzle. So, as you reflect on your answers, do so with kindness and an open mind. This is not about labeling yourself but about understanding and nurturing your mental well-being. Let's embrace this journey with compassion and curiosity, one question at a time.

II

Your 100 Eye-opening Yes Or No Questions About Your Mental Health

Chapter 1: Stress and Anxiety

The Daily Grind of Emma

Emma's alarm blares at 6:30 AM, jolting her awake. She lies in bed, her mind racing with the day's tasks even before her feet hit the floor. Work deadlines, bills to pay, and a never-ending to-do list swirl in her head like a relentless storm. On the subway, her heart races as she mentally rehearses her presentation. At work, while her colleagues chat over coffee, Emma's thoughts are elsewhere, tangled in a web of what-ifs and worst-case scenarios. Her days blur into a relentless cycle of worry and exhaustion.

Have you ever felt like Emma? Overwhelmed by daily responsibilities and haunted by constant worries?

Understanding Stress and Anxiety

Stress and anxiety are not just buzzwords; they're realities that affect countless individuals. They can creep up silently, tightening their grip on your life, often without warning. But what if you could recognize their signs and gently steer your life away from their grasp?

The Invisible Weight

For Emma, stress is like an invisible weight she carries. It's there when she's reviewing her work, when she's trying to relax, even when she's laughing with friends. Anxiety, on the other hand, is like an uninvited guest, popping up at the most inconvenient times, making her question her every decision.

Do you recognize these feelings? Do they visit you often, making your days heavier and your nights restless?

The Power of Reflection

The journey to understanding and managing stress and anxiety begins with reflection. Asking the right questions can be a powerful first step. It's not about finding immediate answers but about starting a conversation with yourself.

Your Personal Exploration

As you read through the following questions, picture yourself in your daily life. Think about the moments that make you tense and the thoughts that stir unease. Be honest with yourself, but also be kind. Remember, this is not about judging but about understanding.

1. Do you often feel overwhelmed by your responsibilities?
2. Do you worry about the future frequently?
3. Do you find it hard to relax?

4. Does your heart race, or do you feel sweaty in stressful situations?
5. Do you avoid certain situations because they make you anxious?
6. Do you often feel nervous or on edge?
7. Do you have difficulty concentrating because of your worries?
8. Do you experience physical symptoms like headaches when stressed?
9. Do you find it hard to control your worries?
10. Do you feel like you're always on high alert?

* * *

Through this chapter, the goal is not to solve all your stress and anxiety issues but to start a meaningful dialogue with yourself. To recognize, reflect, and gently nudge your life toward a calmer, more centered existence. Like Emma, you may not eliminate stress and anxiety overnight, but understanding them is the beginning of a healthier, more balanced life.

Exercise #1

Exercise: Stress Awareness

At the end of each day for the next week, take 10 minutes to write down moments when you felt stressed or anxious. Don't analyze or judge; just note them down. Over the next week, you'll start to see patterns. This awareness is your first step toward managing stress and anxiety.

Chapter 2: Mood and Emotions

In the World of Michael

Michael sits quietly at his desk, gazing out the window. The sky is a canvas of soft blues and pinks, yet he feels a storm brewing inside him. Just yesterday, he was the life of the party, his laughter the loudest. But today, his world seems colorless. He wonders why these sudden shifts in mood happen and why joy and sadness dance so closely in his life.

Have you ever felt like Michael? Riding the unpredictable waves of emotions, feeling vibrant one moment and desolate the next?

The Ebb and Flow of Emotions

Mood and emotions are like the weather—ever-changing, sometimes predictable, often surprising. They paint our days in different shades, influencing how we see the world and interact with others.

Navigating Emotional Seas

For Michael, understanding these mood swings is like trying to navigate a boat in uncharted waters. Some days the sea is calm; other days, waves of emotion threaten to overturn his boat. But what if he could learn to read these emotional currents and sail more smoothly through them?

Do you recognize this in your own life? Are there moments when emotions take the helm, steering you in directions you hadn't planned?

Asking the Right Questions

The journey to emotional awareness is paved with questions. These questions aren't about right or wrong answers; they're about peeling back layers and exploring the depths of your emotional world.

Your Emotional Compass

As you ponder these questions, allow yourself to be both the navigator and the explorer of your emotional seas. Be honest but gentle with yourself as you chart this personal journey.

1. Do you often feel sad or down without any specific reason?
2. Do you have sudden mood swings?
3. Do you struggle to find joy in activities you used to enjoy?
4. Do you feel emotionally numb or indifferent frequently?
5. Do you often feel irritable or easily angered?
6. Do you feel hopeless about the future?

7. Do you have a hard time understanding or managing your emotions?
8. Do you often feel guilty without a clear reason?
9. Do you feel disconnected from others emotionally?
10. Do you frequently feel anxious or scared?

* * *

Michael's story, like yours, is a journey of self-discovery. Understanding your emotional landscape isn't about controlling every feeling; it's about recognizing, embracing, and navigating them with greater awareness. By engaging with these questions and exercises, you're taking the first step toward emotional resilience and a more balanced life.

Exercise #2

Exercise: Emotion Awareness

For the next two weeks, keep a mood diary. Twice a day, jot down your mood and the thoughts accompanying it. Don't judge or analyze; just observe. This exercise will help you become more aware of your emotional patterns and triggers.

Chapter 3: Self-Esteem and Confidence

Sara's Reflections

Sara stands before the mirror, her gaze fixed but her mind wandering. In her reflection, she sees a person filled with potential, yet doubts whisper loudly in her ears. At work, she hesitates to voice her ideas, fearing they're not good enough. In social gatherings, she shrinks back, overshadowed by a nagging sense of inadequacy. She longs to break free from these chains of self-doubt and embrace confidence.

Can you relate to Sara? Have you ever felt like you weren't good enough because of your own self-criticism?

The Journey of Self-Worth

Self-esteem and confidence are the silent narrators of our life stories. They color our perceptions and shape our interactions. Yet, often, we're unaware of their influence, moving through life tuned into a frequency of self-doubt.

Echoes of Doubt

For Sara, each day is a battle against these echoes of doubt. They question her worth, challenge her capabilities, and cast shadows on her achievements. But what if she could tune into a different narrative, one that speaks of strength, capability, and worth?

Do you hear similar echoes? Do you find yourself shying away from opportunities, not because they're out of reach but because you feel you're not worthy of them?

Questioning to Understand

To shift the narrative, we must start by asking ourselves the right questions. These questions aren't about criticism; they're about curiosity and understanding. They're the first step in acknowledging and then rewriting the story of our self-worth.

Discovering Your True Self

As you explore these questions, let them be a mirror, reflecting your true self. Approach them with openness and honesty, and be prepared to see yourself in a new light.

1. Do you often feel inadequate or not good enough?
2. Do you struggle to accept compliments?
3. Do you frequently compare yourself negatively to others?
4. Do you doubt your ability to complete tasks?
5. Do you feel undeserving of happiness or success?
6. Do you have a negative image of your body or appearance?
7. Do you often need others' approval to feel good about

yourself?

8. Do you shy away from challenges because you fear failure?
9. Do you feel like an impostor in your achievements?
10. Do you criticize yourself harshly for your mistakes?

* * *

Sara's story is a journey toward self-acceptance and empowerment, much like your own. By engaging with these questions and exercises, you're not just exploring your self-esteem; you're nurturing it. Remember, confidence is not about never feeling doubt; it's about not letting that doubt define you. As you turn the pages of your own story, let each chapter be written with a stronger sense of self-worth and belief.

Exercise #3

Exercise: Self-appreciation

For the next month, start each day by writing down three things you appreciate about yourself. They can be qualities, achievements, or even simple acts of kindness you've done. This daily practice will help cultivate a more positive self-view and strengthen your confidence.

Chapter 4: Social Interaction and Relationships

Alex's Quiet Corner

In a bustling café, Alex sits quietly in a corner, sipping coffee and observing the lively conversations around him. He often finds himself on the periphery of social gatherings, enveloped in a bubble of solitude. While he longs to connect, a wall of uncertainty holds him back. His mind buzzes with questions about what to say, how to act, and the fear of being judged.

Does this sound familiar to you? Have you ever felt like an outsider, watching life happen from the sidelines?

The Dance of Social Interactions

Social interactions and relationships are intricate dances we perform daily. They shape our connections, our sense of belonging, and our place in the world. For some, like Alex, this dance feels awkward, filled with missteps and uncertainty.

The Barrier of Discomfort

Alex's discomfort in social settings is like an invisible barrier. It separates him from the warmth of relationships and the joy of connection. He wonders what it would be like to cross this barrier, engage effortlessly, and build meaningful relationships.

Do you see parts of yourself in Alex? Do you struggle to bridge the gap between wanting to connect and actually doing it?

Asking the Right Questions

Understanding our social selves starts with introspection. By asking ourselves thoughtful questions, we begin to unravel the complexities of our social interactions and relationships.

Your Social Self-Exploration

As you read these questions, reflect on your own experiences in social settings. Think about your interactions, your relationships, and your feelings about them. Be honest in your reflections, but also be compassionate with yourself.

1. Do you find it hard to make or maintain friendships?
2. Do you often feel uncomfortable at social gatherings?
3. Do you prefer to avoid meeting new people?
4. Do you feel lonely even when you are with others?
5. Do you find it difficult to trust others?
6. Do you often feel misunderstood by people around you?
7. Do you hesitate to express your opinions in a group?
8. Do you feel drained after social interactions?

9. Do you worry about being rejected or judged in social settings?
10. Do you feel like you don't belong or fit in with others?

* * *

Alex's journey of social discovery mirrors the challenges many face in forging connections. This chapter isn't just about becoming more social; it's about understanding your social self and nurturing your relationships. Remember, the quality of our connections often reflects the quality of our lives. As you step out of your comfort zone, do so with the knowledge that each interaction is a step toward a richer, more connected life.

Exercise #4

Exercise: Your Social Comfort

For the next two weeks, challenge yourself to initiate at least one social interaction each day. It could be a simple greeting to a neighbor, a chat with a colleague, or a call to a friend. Note down how you felt before, during, and after each interaction. This exercise aims to gradually increase your comfort in social settings.

Chapter 5: Sleep Patterns and Energy Levels

Liam's Endless Nights

Liam stares at the ceiling, the clock ticking loudly in the quiet of the night. It's past midnight, and sleep eludes him again. His mind races with thoughts from the day and worries for tomorrow, making each minute feel like an hour. When morning comes, he's drained, his energy sapped before the day even begins.

Does this resonate with you? Do you find yourself tossing and turning at night, only to face the day feeling exhausted?

The Cycle of Sleep and Energy

Sleep is the unsung hero of our daily lives, a foundational pillar for our well-being. For Liam, like many others, disrupted sleep patterns and low energy levels have become a frustrating norm.

The Quest for Restful Nights

Liam's quest is not just for sleep but for restorative rest. Nights that rejuvenate and days filled with vitality seem like distant dreams. He wonders what it would take to break this cycle and embrace mornings with energy and enthusiasm.

Do you share Liam's struggle? Do you yearn for nights of peaceful slumber and days of unflagging energy?

Unraveling Sleep Mysteries

Understanding our sleep patterns and energy levels begins with introspection. Asking ourselves honest questions can shed light on our nightly rituals and daily vigor (or lack thereof).

Reflecting on Your Rest

As you contemplate these questions, think about your own sleep habits and how they affect your day-to-day life. Be honest in your assessment, but approach it with an attitude of self-care and improvement.

1. Do you struggle to fall asleep or stay asleep?
2. Do you often feel tired, even after a full night's sleep?
3. Do you rely on substances like caffeine to stay awake during the day?
4. Do you find your sleep pattern to be irregular or disrupted?
5. Do you frequently feel too tired to engage in daily activities?
6. Do you wake up feeling unrefreshed or groggy?
7. Do you take naps during the day because you feel ex-

hausted?

8. Do you have nightmares or disturbing dreams regularly?
9. Do you find it hard to get out of bed in the morning?
10. Do you feel like you need more sleep than most people?

* * *

Liam's story is a common narrative in our fast-paced world. This chapter isn't just about finding sleep solutions; it's about understanding your body's needs and rhythms. Remember, quality sleep is not a luxury; it's a necessity for a healthy, energetic life. As you turn the pages of your own sleep journey, do so with the intent to embrace rest as a vital part of your well-being.

Exercise #5

Exercise: Identify Your Sleep Patterns

For the next month, maintain a sleep diary. Record the time you go to bed, the approximate time it takes you to fall asleep, your night awakenings, and the time you wake up. Also, note your energy levels at different times during the day. This record will help you identify patterns and take steps toward improving your sleep and energy levels.

Chapter 6: Coping Mechanisms

Jenna's Balancing Act

Jenna sits at her kitchen table, a cup of tea cooling untouched as her mind races through a maze of challenges. Work stress, family demands, personal goals—it's like juggling balls in the air, trying not to let one drop. She often turns to late-night TV binges or mindless scrolling through social media, hoping to distract herself from the stress, but these strategies rarely bring peace or solutions.

Can you relate to Jenna's story? How do you cope when life throws curveballs your way?

The Art of Coping

Coping mechanisms are our mental and emotional tools, our strategies for dealing with life's ups and downs. For Jenna, and perhaps for you too, finding effective and healthy ways to cope is a constant struggle.

Seeking Solace in the Storm

Jenna's coping strategies are like temporary shelters in a storm. They offer momentary relief, but the storm still rages on. She wonders what it would be like to face the storm head-on, armed with healthier, more resilient coping mechanisms.

Do you find yourself in a similar situation? Are your coping strategies more about escaping than confronting?

Exploring Your Coping Toolbox

To build a robust coping toolbox, we must first understand the tools we currently use. This understanding begins with asking ourselves some direct yet compassionate questions.

Reflecting on Your Resilience

As you consider these questions, think about how you've handled recent challenges. Remember, this isn't about judgment but about awareness and growth.

1. Do you often use alcohol or drugs to cope with your feelings?
2. Do you avoid facing problems by distracting yourself?
3. Do you find it hard to talk about your feelings with others?
4. Do you engage in compulsive behaviors like overeating or shopping to feel better?
5. Do you isolate yourself when you're upset or stressed?
6. Do you often feel overwhelmed when faced with a problem?
7. Do you struggle to find solutions to the challenges you face?

8. Do you ignore or suppress your feelings rather than dealing with them?
9. Do you find yourself getting angry or upset when coping with stress?
10. Do you often feel helpless or unable to cope with life's challenges?

* * *

Jenna's journey, like yours, is about building resilience and finding strength in adversity. This chapter isn't merely about coping; it's about transforming your coping mechanisms into powerful tools for handling life's complexities. Remember, the way we cope can either be a path to growth or an obstacle to it. As you explore your own methods of coping, do so with the goal of nurturing resilience and empowering yourself to face life's challenges head-on.

Exercise #6

Exercise: Coping Mechanisms Awareness

Over the next two weeks, observe and write down your reactions to stressful or challenging situations. Next to each entry, note if the reaction was constructive or if it was an escape or avoidance. This exercise aims to increase your awareness of your coping mechanisms and encourage the development of healthier strategies.

Chapter 7: Thought Patterns

Ethan's Mind Maze

Ethan lounges on his sofa, a book in hand, yet his eyes glaze over the pages. His mind is a battlefield of thoughts—some uplifting, many self-defeating. He wonders why his brain often defaults to the worst-case scenarios or dwells on past mistakes. "Is it just me?" he ponders, "or does everyone have this constant mental chatter?"

Does Ethan's internal struggle sound familiar? Do you find yourself caught in a similar whirlpool of thoughts, both positive and negative?

Navigating the Mind's Labyrinth

Our thought patterns are the architects of our reality. They shape our perceptions, influence our decisions, and color our emotions. For Ethan, understanding and navigating these patterns feels like walking through a labyrinth with no clear exit.

The Echoes of Thoughts

Ethan's mind echoes with a mixture of thoughts: some are rational and constructive, while others are irrational and debilitating. He seeks clarity amidst this cacophony, yearning for a balance that favors positive, rational thinking.

Do you recognize this in your life? Are your thoughts your allies, guiding you wisely, or do they sometimes feel like adversaries, leading you astray?

Questioning the Mind's Pathways

To gain insight into our thought processes, we must engage in self-inquiry. By asking ourselves purposeful questions, we can begin to understand the nature of our thoughts and their impact on our lives.

Your Mental Exploration

As you ponder these questions, reflect on your own thought patterns. Be honest but gentle with yourself, understanding that this is a journey of self-discovery and growth.

1. Do you often expect the worst to happen?
2. Do you struggle to let go of negative thoughts?
3. Do you find yourself overthinking about past events?
4. Do you often criticize yourself in your thoughts?
5. Do you have trouble thinking positively about the future?
6. Do you feel like your thoughts are often out of your control?
7. Do you dwell on your mistakes or failures?

8. Do you believe that others are judging you negatively?
9. Do you feel like your mind is constantly racing?
10. Do you often feel confused or struggle to make decisions?

43

* * *

Ethan's journey through his mind's labyrinth is a quest for mental clarity and peace, much like your own. This chapter isn't about silencing your thoughts; it's about understanding and harmonizing them. Remember, the nature of your thoughts greatly influences the quality of your life. As you delve into your own thought patterns, do so with the aim of cultivating a more positive, rational, and peaceful mind.

Exercise #7

Exercise: Thought Patterns

For the next month, practice mindfulness meditation for 10 minutes each day. Focus on your breath and observe your thoughts without judgment or engagement. This exercise can help you become more aware of your thought patterns and learn to gently steer them toward positivity and rationality.

Chapter 8: Lifestyle and Habits

Grace's Daily Dance

The sun peeks through the blinds, casting a warm glow over Grace's room. She stirs, groggy, and reluctant to start the day. Her morning routine is a haphazard dance of snooze buttons, rushed coffee, and skipped breakfasts. Evenings are no different—a blend of screen time, takeout dinners, and late hours. Grace knows these habits aren't serving her well, but breaking free from their grasp feels daunting.

Do you see reflections of your own life in Grace's story? Are your daily habits supporting your mental health, or are they barriers to your well-being?

The Tapestry of Habits

Our habits are the threads that weave the tapestry of our daily lives. They are the small choices we make consistently, shaping our health, mood, and overall well-being. For Grace, as perhaps for you, these habits have become ingrained patterns, challenging to alter but not impossible.

Rethinking Routine

Grace's daily routine is a comfort zone, albeit a flawed one. It's familiar, yet it leaves her feeling depleted and unfulfilled. She yearns for change, for habits that nourish her body and mind.

Are you in a similar place? Are you looking to transform your routines into stepping stones for better mental health?

Unraveling the Habitual Knots

Understanding and reshaping our habits starts with honest introspection. By asking ourselves the right questions, we can begin to untangle the knots of our daily routines and reweave them into healthier patterns.

Exploring Your Daily Rhythms

As you ponder these questions, think about your daily routines and habits. Approach this reflection with an open mind and a willingness to embrace change.

1. Do you spend most of your day sitting or inactive?
2. Do you find it hard to maintain a healthy diet?
3. Do you often skip meals or eat irregularly?
4. Do you find it difficult to stick to a routine?
5. Do you spend a lot of time on screens (phone, computer, TV)?
6. Do you neglect self-care activities like grooming or dressing?
7. Do you often engage in activities that you know are un-

healthy?

8. Do you struggle to make time for relaxation or hobbies?
9. Do you frequently stay up late, even when you're tired?
10. Do you neglect physical exercise?

* * *

Grace's story is about transformation—transforming everyday habits into a foundation for mental and physical health. This chapter isn't just about identifying unhealthy habits; it's about initiating positive changes that resonate through all aspects of your life. Remember, each small habit changed is a step toward a healthier, happier you. As you embark on this journey, do so with patience and persistence, knowing that every effort counts in crafting a better lifestyle.

Exercise #8

Exercise: For a Healthier Lifestyle

For the next month, choose one habit you wish to change or improve. Set small, achievable goals for this change. Each week, evaluate your progress and adjust your approach if needed. This focused effort can help you gradually incorporate healthier habits into your lifestyle.

Chapter 9: Work-Life Balance

Tom's Tightrope Walk

Tom's life feels like a perpetual tightrope walk. Balancing a demanding job and personal life is like juggling fire—exhilarating yet exhausting. His weekends are usually spent catching up on work, with his weekdays being a blur of meetings and deadlines. A persistent sense of guilt or the pull of his inbox obscures the rare moments of leisure. "Is this what success feels like?" Tom often wonders.

Does Tom's story echo your experiences? Do you find yourself struggling to maintain equilibrium between your professional and personal life?

The Elusive Balance

Achieving work-life balance is akin to finding the elusive golden mean—a state of equilibrium where neither work nor personal life overwhelms the other. For Tom, and perhaps for you, this balance seems like a distant, almost unattainable dream.

The Weight of Work

Tom's professional life, while rewarding, feels like a heavyweight, tipping the scales against his personal time and relationships. He craves a sense of harmony, where work is a part of his life, not the entirety of it.

Do you feel similarly burdened? Is your work encroaching on your personal time, leaving you feeling depleted and disconnected from your own life?

Reflecting on Your Scales

To find balance, we must first understand where the imbalance lies. This understanding begins with asking ourselves honest, sometimes difficult, questions.

Assessing Your Balance

As you read these questions, reflect on your own life. Think about how you allocate your time and energy between work and personal pursuits. Approach this self-assessment with a desire for harmony and well-being.

1. Do you often bring work home or think about work in your free time?
2. Do you feel like your work is taking over your personal life?
3. Do you find it hard to take breaks or vacations from work?
4. Do you often work long hours or overtime?
5. Do you feel guilty when you are not working?
6. Do you struggle to find time for family or friends because

of work?

7. Do you find it difficult to say no to work-related requests?

8. Do you feel stressed about work even during your off-hours?

9. Do you neglect your hobbies or personal interests due to work?

10. Do you feel like your work is affecting your health or happiness?

* * *

Tom's story is a common narrative in our fast-paced, work-centric world. This chapter isn't just about reducing work hours; it's about creating a life where work and personal time coexist harmoniously. Remember, work-life balance is not a static state but a dynamic process of adjustment and realignment. As you navigate your own balancing act, do so with the understanding that both aspects of your life are vital and deserve attention and care.

Exercise #9

Exercise: Work-Life Balance

For the next two weeks, consciously allocate specific times for work and personal activities. During personal time, resist the urge to check work emails or think about work-related tasks. At the end of the two weeks, evaluate how this separation has affected your sense of balance and well-being.

Chapter 10: Physical Health and Wellness

Nadia's Forgotten Foundation

Nadia, a vibrant and creative soul, often forgets that her body is the foundation upon which her life is built. With a busy schedule and a focus on career and family, her physical health often takes a backseat. Skipping meals, irregular sleep, and minimal exercise have become the norm. Yet she wonders why she feels mentally drained and emotionally off-balance.

Does Nadia's story resonate with you? Have you considered how your physical health might be intertwined with your mental well-being?

The Body-Mind Connection

Physical health and mental well-being are intricately linked; they are two sides of the same coin. For Nadia, as perhaps for you, neglecting physical health has subtle yet profound effects on mental state and emotional stability.

Overlooking the Essentials

Nadia's oversight is not uncommon. In the hustle of daily life, it's easy to overlook the essentials: nutrition, sleep, and exercise. But these are not just boxes to be checked; they are pillars supporting our overall well-being.

Do you find yourself making similar oversights? Are you underestimating the impact of physical health on your mental and emotional life?

A Deeper Look at Health

Understanding the connection between physical health and mental well-being begins with self-reflection. By asking ourselves pertinent questions, we can uncover how our lifestyle choices are influencing our overall health.

Exploring Your Health Habits

As you consider these questions, reflect on your daily health habits. Approach this self-exploration with honesty, and remember, the goal is not self-criticism but self-awareness and improvement.

1. Do you often ignore physical symptoms or delay seeking medical help?
2. Do you feel like your physical health is not a priority?
3. Do you experience frequent physical discomfort or pain?
4. Do you find it difficult to maintain regular health check-ups?

5. Do you neglect physical activities or exercises?
6. Do you often eat fast food or unhealthy snacks?
7. Do you ignore advice or instructions from healthcare professionals?
8. Do you struggle with managing chronic health conditions?
9. Do you feel like your physical health is affecting your mental well-being?
10. Do you avoid activities that could improve your physical health?

* * *

Nadia's journey to rediscover her physical foundation is a reminder of the holistic nature of health. This chapter isn't just about physical fitness; it's about recognizing the deep connection between our bodies and our minds. Remember, nurturing your physical health is not a separate task from caring for your mental well-being; they are complementary and equally vital. As you embark on this journey, do so with the understanding that caring for your body is a fundamental act of self-love and respect.

Exercise #10

Exercise: Physical Health and Wellness

For the next month, set three small but significant health goals, perhaps related to diet, sleep, and exercise. Each week, track your progress and reflect on how these changes are affecting your mental and emotional state. This practice can help highlight the profound impact of physical health on your overall well-being.

What Is Your Result?

How many Yes or No answers do you have?

Yes =

No =

Are You Mentally Ok?

What are your thoughts?

Now WHAT? You May Ask

So, you have counted the number of yes and no answers, interpreted the result, and come up with the ultimate answer. **Now WHAT? You May Ask**

You've journeyed through the pages, answered the questions, and tallied up the 'yeses' and 'noes'. The patterns have emerged, perhaps clearer than you expected, or maybe they've left you with more questions. So, now what? What do you do with this newfound understanding of your mental landscape? This chapter is dedicated to guiding you on the next steps after unveiling the ultimate answer about your mental well-being.

Firstly, take a moment to acknowledge the effort you've put in. Engaging with these questions isn't just an activity; it's a brave step toward self-awareness. Whether your answers leaned toward 'yes' or 'no', each one has contributed to a deeper understanding of yourself. But understanding is just the beginning. What comes next is equally, if not more, important. How do you translate this understanding into action?

If you've discovered areas of your mental health that are flourishing, that's fantastic! Celebrate these strengths. Could these areas of positivity be leveraged to improve aspects of your life that are less robust? For instance, if you have a high degree of self-esteem, could this be a foundation to address areas like stress management or emotional regulation?

On the flip side, if you've identified aspects that need attention, this is not a cause for alarm but an opportunity for growth. Each 'no' is not a setback but a signpost pointing toward areas for improvement. The key question now is: how can you address these areas? Is it through seeking professional help, engaging in self-care practices, or maybe starting a conversation with a trusted friend or family member?

Remember, this book is not the end of your journey; it's a tool to help you navigate the complexities of your mental health. The ultimate answer you've arrived at is not a final destination. It's a compass pointing you toward the next steps, be they further exploration, seeking help, or building on your strengths.

Moreover, it's essential to approach these next steps with kindness and patience. Mental health is not a static state; it's a continuous process of growth and change. The insights you've gained today are a snapshot of where you are now, not where you'll always be. Can you give yourself the grace to grow and evolve at your own pace?

In conclusion, having counted your 'yeses' and 'noes' and interpreted the results, the question of 'Now what?' opens the door to a myriad of possibilities. This is where you take the insights and turn them into action. Whether it's building on your strengths, addressing your challenges, or simply continuing the journey of self-discovery, each step is valuable. So, take a deep breath, embrace the journey ahead with an open heart, and remember, you're not alone on this path. Each step you take is a step toward a more aware, healthier you.

Conclusion: A Heartfelt Thank You

A Heartfelt Thank You and A Gentle Request

As we reach the conclusion, "Are You Mentally OK?" I want to extend a heartfelt thank you. Your decision to purchase and read this book is not just a testament to your commitment to personal growth and mental well-being, but it's also a step toward spreading awareness about the importance of mental health. Your engagement and willingness to embark on this journey of self-discovery are both commendable and deeply appreciated.

Your journey through these pages is more than just an individual experience; it's part of a larger movement toward understanding and prioritizing mental health. By choosing to engage with this book, you've joined a community of individuals who recognize the significance of mental well-being in our lives. This shared journey is a powerful one, and its impact can reach far beyond our individual experiences.

Now, I have a gentle request to make. If you found value in this book and if it has provided you with insights, comfort, or guidance, I encourage you to leave a review. Your feedback is not just valuable to me as the author, but it's also incredibly important for others who might be considering this book. Your review could be the beacon that guides someone else to this resource, someone who might be seeking the very insights and understanding that you've gained.

Think of your review as a ripple in a pond, extending the reach of the book's message. Each opinion, each shared experience, contributes to a larger narrative about the importance of mental health. By leaving a review, you're not just offering your perspective; you're helping to amplify a message that is crucial in our current times.

Reviews also play a critical role in making books more visible and accessible to a wider audience. In the vast ocean of literature, it's easy for important messages to be lost. Your review can help ensure that this book reaches the hands of those who might need it most, those who are perhaps on the brink of starting their own journey toward better mental health.

So, I kindly ask you to take a few moments to leave a review. Share your thoughts, your experiences, and how this book has impacted you. Your words have the power to inspire, encourage, and guide others who might be seeking a path toward understanding their mental health.

Thank you once again for joining me on this journey. The path to mental well-being is a continuous one, filled with learning, growth, and self-discovery. May the insights you've gained from this book stay with you and serve as a guiding light in your journey. Remember, your mental health is a precious gift, and nurturing it is one of the most important journeys you can embark on.

With gratitude and best wishes for your continued journey,

Yakalou